Know When The Spirit Speaks

Faith Going In

Annette Alexander

Know When The Spirit Speaks

Faith Going In

Scripture quotations, unless otherwise indicated, are taken from the *Holy Bible, King James Version*, Cambridge, 1769. Used by permission. All rights reserved.

The opinions expressed by the author are not necessarily those of Fountain of Life Publishers House.

Published by Fountain of Life Publishers House
P. O. Box 922612 Norcross, GA 30010
404-936-3989
Please Email Manuscripts to: publish@pariceparker.biz

Fountain of Life Publishing House is committed to excellence in the publishing industry. The Company reflects the philosophy established by the founder, based on Psalm 68:11, "The Lord gave the word and great was the company of those who published it."

Book design copyright © 2015 by Fountain of Life Publishers House. All rights reserved.
Cover Design by Parice Parker
Interior design by Phyllis R Brown
Editor: Lorraine Hopkins

Published in the United States of America

ISBN: 978-0-9904441-2-1

January 5, 2014

Faith Going In

Fountain of Life Publishers House

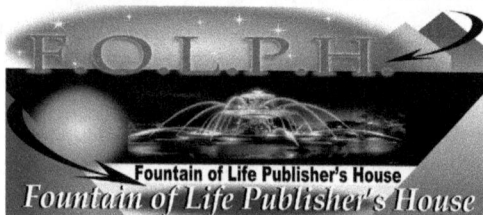

For book orders or wholesale distribution
Website: www.pariceparker.biz

Annette Alexander

Faith Going In

What Inspired This Book?

One day I met an administrator at the elementary school my daughter Mikezia attended. I was telling her about the business that I was starting and at that time she was my listener. I paid my friend $2000.00 to write my policies and procedures for a Home Health Care Service, but she never gave them to me; so instead I opened Faith Cleaning Services, Incorporated.

I always told myself Faith Home Care Services will be reserved until the time comes for the plan. During our conversation I explained to her what God was doing in my life. She had already begun to see change begin in me. As I shared some details about my life; I told her I was going to write a book. That day was so gloomy. So she handed me a flier with Parice Parker's information about a free creative writing seminar. I called and spoke with Ms. Parker. I was able to share my thoughts after her creative writing seminar was over, at the

Library on North Tryon Street in Charlotte, North Carolina. Since then my hands and mind have gotten to work. As I followed GOD specific instructions. I discovered a long season of trials, tribulation, setbacks, and lack. The more I followed God, the more the enemy had to LET ME GO. I love new things especially something benefiting to me. I want to THANK GOD and all the people that helped me through this journey. I would not have completed the task if it was not for the saints and the sinners!

Annette Alexander

Faith Going In

Table of Contents

Introduction

Annette Alexander

Faith Going In

Introduction

I realized I have a gift; a jewel in hand. I must use them to the fullest. My hands are useful for the task. As a child I wanted to sing, but no one knew. I did not make it known. One day I was supposed to be in a talent show; however, because of fear I backed out. I had no one to encourage me. Lost dreams can pass you by. I was plagued with fear and doubt in my life then sin begin to enter. As I matured, a determination of change came over me. I tried everything I knew and still came up with nothing to show for it. The wrong set of keys is what I had, but when I switched my keys into the Kingdom then doors began to open and close. When everyone walked out "GOD" stepped in because I had the **FAITH GOING IN.**

Annette Alexander

Chapter One

When It Is Time!

God can change things in the blink of an eye. So be on the lookout for your "BLESSINGS!" Remember do not give up because you never know when your light will have to shine and do not let disappointments stop you. You cannot do anything about the past. Haran means, "No more wasted years." A lot of people have been stuck to long. Now, it is time to move forward. GOD will strengthen you to be obedient. God is using me for this appointed time. I pray this book; "Faith Going In," is a great tool to help you conquer. Therefore, your gifts and talents will not lay dormant. Complacency will never amount to anything in this world. One thing I have learned is all things are possible. Therefore, while you have breath, put your mind to use and gain wisdom to obtain your dreams. Peace and Blessings awaits Obedience. I thank You Lord that You do not remember my iniquity or sins and have taken away my wrath, sickness and disease. Oh, how I Love You Jesus. Hear my prayers. I have been restored! **Amen.** My desire is to mature people and provide encouraging SPIRIT to SPIRIT messages. The words that I speak are Spirit and Life. Receive the Spirited Words of Life. Be sure whatever is in your Spirit is what God say's. This message that My Heavenly Father has prepared is BIGGER than a BOOK. I have wasted valuable LIFE, but do not focus on the negative, and do not live locked out of life. Change the channel and choose to live life right!

Psalms 37:4
Delight yourself also in the Lord; and He shall give you the desires of your heart.

Spiritual is when you can forgive someone even when they use you. Many are being destroyed daily; letting what others say rule their lives and kill their joy. Everyone is not going to understand you, sooner or later they are going to find fault in you. I have an assignment to develop my task and I must refocus my life to get it done. Cut the distractions. I WAS NOT created for you to like me, but to LOVE Me. My goal is to represent God in this earth so people can see Him through me. We are to:

EPHESIANS 5:1

"therefore be imitators of God as dear children, run with purpose in every step and go out each day with a goal."

If you do not stop trying you can never fail. Always go the extra mile. We live too much for people and not enough for our LORD and SAVIOR. You have to follow the Leadership of the Holy Spirit. We need Leaders who stand up and stand out. As Christians we must grow. We need to be richly developed in WISDOM. Christianity requires growth in faith and belief, not another mythology Religion or Domination. The LORD needs you to use your gifts He has instilled in you for the up building of His kingdom on earth. A man's hearts must bow down to God. We need to become greater seekers of the kingdom. Christ is looking for true worshipers and His search is unlimited! He is coming to bring a new paradise on earth; so get on the ban wagon. Surely my Father wants my life to be a testimony. Make your walk with Jesus exciting and fulfilling because He wants us to forever be with Him and also to maintain happiness.

JOHN 14:6

Jesus answered, "I am the way the truth and the life."

His way comes to replace our identity and His identity comes to replace our character. The mind of God is to make us in the likeness of Him.

Undeveloped Christians live below their means because many do not want to listen; neither follow directions or like to be told what to do, when to do it, or how. A lot of people practice fighting, holding grudges and/or being angry. This will not cause you to get ahead; it will only hold you back. Going against another will only keep you behind and that is not of God. We have to become real about ourselves. I am playing catch-up! I have decided to follow Jesus and now there is no turning back! You will be safe in His hands and Hell must be dismissed out of your life. Though you may experience struggles and troubles, do not give up on God. He is turning all your bad into good, but you cannot give up on going forth.

I am on a journey. We have to stay stirred up on this journey. I need someone that will pull their self-close to me and I can also help them. Iron sharpens iron and it is best to associate with those that are striving in the right direction. It will help you stay more focused. God wants to put someone close to you in your life. We are supposed to live our lives to be a Blessing to others. Get your mind off of yourself. What am I doing to help others? If you want to stay alive and continue to grow you have to remain teachable. Let God teach you something; then, go out in the world and demonstrate it. To be perfected - You have to go deeper and deeper in Christ. Know that you are not perfect, but you Worship the one who is perfect. You have to please God. I am getting ready to have unstoppable Miracles. Obedience is proof and instruction is the first sign.

"Honor is the seed for ABUNDANCE and dishonor is the seed to PERISH."

Your future is determined by who you honor. If you fail in your life; it will be because of a person you chose to dishonor. You will succeed once you choose to honor and respect that individual God has assigned in your life, to help cultivate your destiny. Abundance is not for all only the ones who honor their instructor. God will allow people in our lives for a purpose and we must respect their strength of mind. Once we achieve that simple task; He will drive us through to our path of abundance. In doing so we can reap our hearts desire, which will push us forward! (Who are you?)

DEUTERONOMY 5:16

"Honor your father and mother, as the LORD your God has commanded you, that your days may be long, and that it may be well with you in the land, which the LORD your God is giving you."

Wednesday, March 24, 2010 at 9:21 PM

My heart is broken. I feel empty inside because I am missing the word from God. Sitting here after realizing I need a word from the LORD and debating on what to do?

14

I already know what to do, but do not know how. He can empower you and His word is my strength. I grow weak without Him. I need a fresh anointing to come and heal my land. The anointing is for winning. During my down moments the Lord uplifts me. It was like a dark cloud hanging over my head and I just needed a fresh anointing.

Why wait on someone else when you know what to do and how to do it. Nobody can treat or love me like You, Lord. Always acknowledge Him because He will never leave you neither forsake you. After all He is the only one that has you covered. Listen to the master and believe. He rose for me and He is coming back for us like a thief in the night. I am still growing, as I am just a babe in Christ. Every source of knowledge is accounted for your life when you are doing spiritual purpose. Lord, I need to feel the touch of your hand. Ladies take your place we are more than legs, thighs, and hips. Women we think that is what makes us stand out. It is supposed to be the God in us that people can see. There are times when we do not know how we are going to make it through. We should know if there is a will, there is a way.

Sometimes we will get in a wrong relationship, but through it all I have learned great lessons. Taking back your life gives you purpose to hope again and I regained my freedom when I took my life back. I just begin to call on Jesus instead of who I thought would be there for me. Jesus was my helper before I met the wrong people. Nevertheless, I found out the hard way. He is my helper when they are not there. He will become the biggest of your needs, more than anything on this earth when your life comes down to the wire. Asking you this very familiar question? Who is for me, and who is against me? Do not compare yourself with others we are not in competition, and may not be called for the same purpose. Yet, our life should shine in spite of our storms. I am going to shine everywhere I go. God knows how to make you look good even in the worse times and loose those things in your life.

HE IS THE GOD OF POWER, LOVE AND A SOUND MIND AND FEAR IS NOT OF HIM

AND FAITH COMES BY HEARING!!!!! WHAT ARE YOU LISTENING TO???????

Every day I am going to claim new territory. I cannot quit because someone is always watching. God can use anyone He chooses. When I give, it is a chance to change people lives. I love to reach out and help others. Always see what you can do for others. Forge ahead and focus on what God has placed in your heart and His words are never ending. Someone is always around to teach us principle's on how we should live. Keep the vision in front of you and soon it will be at your fingertips.

Commitment is so important. It takes a lifetime of prayer and fasting to be powerful in the word of God. It takes a Godly love, for it is Love that gives you power and it covers a multitude of sins. One step at a time! Real commitment requires patience. I fell down plenty of times, but I got right back up with help from above. I kept thriving right in the mist of famine. One must never stop producing fruit. One must thrive through economic downfalls; be fruitful and multiply that is the word from God to us. I can praise in the mist of Hell and Heaven. People need to know God for themselves. He will save you from famine. I cannot settle for less and always want the best QUALITY of everything because hard work pays off if you plan well. We will increase when we stay focused. Obedience is where the blessings are. However, it is something how a lot of people will search in crazy places and all they have to do is obey God. Always keep sowing seeds keep tithing, keep walking by Faith, and keep going to church. Do not let your eyes go dim so that you cannot see your way out of any situation. Do not be mad because you cannot find happiness. If you take time to find Jesus you will find happiness. Persecution comes with the word. Navigate through life because staying in motion soon pays off. Something is always moving and changing. The enemy is mad because you are pushing for higher ground. Work what God has given you while the opportunity is yours. Remember you are a word in motion. Continue to speak positive about your life and speak those things into existence that you do not yet have. GET READY because you are next in line for your miracle. For the things that are seen are temporary. God is going to move you from now to then. The first shall be last and the last shall be first! God is getting ready to position you. He is getting ready to shift things in your life.

For all you LITTLE folks it is time to get BIG! You can have what you want in life. If you just give your life to Christ. Life is full of obstacles and illusions, but you must realize who you are. During the storm be prepared to stand. Only the ones that endure will survive. Maintain your life with God, not the world because He is the one who picks you up.

JUDE 1:7 –

"As Sodom and Gomorrah, and the cities around them in a similar manner to these, having given themselves over to sexual immorality and gone after strange flesh, are set forth as an example, suffering the vengeance of eternal fire."

Chapter Two
Blowing Money

Money is a service to us and it serves you. Money cannot buy LOVE, but many love blowing money. How can you ever save when you are too busy blowing money? So many people have missed plenty of opportunities that knocked at their door after they spent out. Then when the money is gone and the spending ends they do not come around anymore. Advertising is the best way to persuade somebody to spend money they do not have for something we do not need. NEVER spend your money before you get it. Ask God how you should spend the money that He allowed you to make? It would be better if you focus on the finer things in life, do not let the world control you try to control the world. Money is what we work for, so if you keep money on your mind, it is going to be hard for you to think about anything else.

A successful man is a man who makes more money than he can ever spend. I wish I had a dollar for every time that I spent a dollar, because then I would have all my money back. "BLOWING MONEY" Try not to buy things, you do not need, and stop buying things that you do not use, because the things you do not use will never amount to the things you do not buy. "BLOWING MONEY" It takes finances to do the things you need to do. God has a covenant with you. You stepped into my upgrade in paradise. I have expensive circumstances and I do not think money can solve the issue. Money situations can bring you up or down and tear you apart, but God provides our needs through His Riches and Glory so wait on him. People seems to try to distract your way of living when it comes to money One will find out who their friends are very quickly.

Always invest in yourself by choosing more education, which will help your learning. When we stray away from God the struggle begins to manifest and you have to find the right path to get back on course. Do not

Know When The Spirit Speaks

doubt or take a second guess about doing good. Because we were made to give freely our love, our time, or whatever we possess, to be a disciple of Christ. It feels good to be able to give, but we have acted as if it hurts our pockets. We must use our tools. Get rich in the Spirit not of the world. The devil gives and takes away. Exchange the mindset of the flesh, to the spirit. Take control of your life, cause time is like a merry-go-round. Always know when to get on or get off. Work hard to get what you want. Your wealth; it will grow. Plan a structure for life or death, which is your will. Learn to manage the resources God has given you, so he can give you more. We all are managers, but He is the owner. Trust God for any and everything. Live and obey all His commandments and give thanks. He will add balance into your life.

2 Corinthians 9:15 - HCSB

"Thanks are to God for His indescribable gifts such as peace, honesty, tender mercies, love, faithfulness, respect, WISDOM, Spirit of Truth, and Revelation. Think about how God has blessed you just thank Him each day."

PSALM 118:29 - HCSB

Know When The Spirit Speaks

"Give thanks to the Lord for He is good; His faithful love endures forever."

PROVERBS 15:31 - NLT

"If you listen to constructive criticism you will be at home among the wise."

Money can solve a whole lot of problems and it can bring new problems. You can lose friends, relatives and things behind money; including your life. Lessons have to be learned. Jealousy and strife comes with having money. People will always think you are their bank. Without it, you cannot do what you would like to do. When they see you're wearing your Blessing, jealousy is around the corner. Watch out for the trials of confusion and stay close to God so you will be able to wear it since He requires you to wear His charm. You will have people that will need you, so be available to meet their needs. Their purpose is to allow your heart to be put through the test God will make people bless you unexpectedly. The goal is to advance the Kingdom of God and live away from the curse and assist with the resources that are given to us in the significance of the time when it occurs.

"EVIL MAKES ME SICK."

One should have a Mission for Their Money. Refocus money - Doing something to make the money work.

PROVERBS 21:5

" The plans of the diligent lead surely to plenty, But those who is hasty, surely to poverty."

Fruit is the works of the Spirit. The Fruits LOVE, JOY, and PEACE are the visible expressions of the power working. It is the evidence of the power producing it. Witness to me. How do I bear more fruit? You have to be pruned. Pruning is a process that the plant must go through; the Kingdom of God. You have been planted, you are fruitful. They can die because of disease. Everybody seems to take my kindness for weakness. No matter how hard I try to please others the worst it gets. I just woke-up and thought about the situation that really let me know I need to get closer to God rather than to people and please our Father, which is in Heaven. No one wants to see you with any more than they have themselves. The HEAVENLY FATHER is the one who Lifts one up and brings one down. GOD forgive me for not being able to pay my Debt. Jesus will bring people in your life to pay off your debt.

I will seek You more and I will abide in Your commandments and laws all the days of my Life. I WILL PAY MY TITHES AND OFFERINGS. I will use my hands for your purpose. I will depend on God and remember the promises that you have stored up for me. One thing about God He will not make anything too hard for you.

People hate to see you able to do what you want to do when they are unable to do so. I believe when you have enemies they cannot even look you in the eyes.

PSALM 110:1

"THE LORD said to my Lord, "Sit at My right hand, till I make your enemies your footstool."

Money is a Gift from God! First we give, then we save and then we spend. Do it immediately when you get money. Make it automatic - you save more when you do not see it. You have to give in order to receive. If I hold my money, it can mess up my giving.

1ˢᵗ *Timothy 6:10*

"It will be given back to you good measured, pressed down, shaking together AND running over will men give into your bosom. For the love of money is a root of all kinds of evil, for which many have strayed from the faith in their greediness, and pierced themselves through with many sorrows."

Learn about the miracle money God is holding for you! There is hard earned money, true money, miracle money, enough money, and it is all GOD's money. Sometimes when people wants you to give, you do not always have to give to certain people. They're going to be some people mad at you. YOU must know how to work your gift. I am ready to give! We have to be a people he can trust. We have to have the right mind set. Your ministry requires provision. God is talking to a people, He wants to show. Pray against the division and pray for unity of all being on one accord for giving. **MONEY answers all things.** That is Power. God will grant extraordinary provisions when we are obedient. If you can help one person and see how it would make a difference. We cannot hide from what is going on in the world. Continue to help others. Do not stop or give up on your position when given the opportunity. **STUDY PROSPERITY!**

DEUTERONOMY 7:15

"And the Lord will take away from you all sickness, and afflict you with none of the terrible diseases of Egypt which you have known, but will lay them on all those who hate you."

Never come into the presence of the King without something. Learn to wait, teach to wait and understand the fullness of joy. Learn to take advantage of His presence. MONEY LOVES to WORK and it makes you feel good. The attitude of giving: 1) you may give. 2) We need to give. 3) We have the opportunity to give. He will multiply your seed. Everything in your life wants to multiply.

Know When The Spirit Speaks

Many people today are eating their seeds. Lord, help us to understand we must position ourselves. The purpose of us having money is for the Kingdom. God gives us skills, success, controls and promotions. Our Lord wants you to have more. A person can change your life. It is not my job to change anyone. God is the one who changes another, but I choose to be an example for the next generation. Money is anywhere God wants you to be. Money is there for you, when you are in the right place. All blessings come through a train of authority. Get busy, go out look for work. The Lord has work for you. Bring in the harvest. Do not sleep through your harvest. It is waiting on you. We reap our harvest with our mouths. Claim what you need. The job is not too hard. Just be at the right place at the right time. Practice what you speak. People who are entrusted with money need to work smarter. We are not required to be super workers, but do the best we possibly can. We should not over work.

EXODUS 34:21

"Six days you shall work, but on the seventh day you shall rest; in plowing time and in

harvest you shall rest. Millionaires are made at midnight."

MARK 10:25

"It is easier for a camel to go through the eye of a needle than a rich man to enter the kingdom of God. Jehovah will multiply what you have. Miracles are moving toward you or away from you. He moves in distinguish time."

What do you do when you need a miracle?

_____

_____

_____

_____

_____

_____

_____

_____

_____

_____

GENESIS 8:22

"While the earth remains, seed time and harvest, cold and heat, winter and summer, and day and night shall not cease."

God have set me apart from others for His purpose, but deep down in my heart I know people envy for varies reasons. God said, "He would make my enemies my footstool." I love being called and chosen to do the work of the Lord. I realized living for the world will put me further and further behind in my calling and destiny, which God has ordained for me. It is GOD'S purpose FOR ME to be out there in the world as a Light to the Gentiles.

My God has been so good to me and in so many different ways. I know trouble does not last. People can make you lose control if you are not in control. Whatever I am going through; I am still chosen by God. He is the Author and the Finisher of everything that I do all the days of my life. Greater things are yet to come!

The Lord has His way. He is moving everywhere. Be anxious for nothing, pray about everything and worry about nothing.

PSALMS 121:3

"He will not suffer thy foot to be moved."

If the Lord will not suffer it, neither men nor devils can do it. How greatly would they rejoice if they could give us a disgraceful fall, drive us from our position, and bury us out of memory.

PSALMS 103:2 - 3

"If you fail to realize you can be a blessing to others; if you just recognize and forget not all his benefits. Who forgives all our iniquities; who heals all thy diseases"

He has let me know, " if I strive for better", He will give me the Best! I will do the best I can for the rest of my life; seek His face, humble myself, pray and watch for the manifestations. Always remember it is the Lord your God who gives you power to become rich, and He does it to fulfill His promise to your ancestors.

DEUTERONOMY 8:18

"But thou shalt remember the Lord thy God; for it is he that gives the power to get wealth, that he may establish his covenant which he swore unto thy fathers, as it is this day."

Know When The Spirit Speaks

I know My Heavenly Father was really angry with me. I thank you for bringing me out of Egypt (Out of bondage). What I learned just by all the mistakes in life is that folks in the world do not want to have anything to do with you unless you have something to give or when they CANNOT EXCEPT THE CHANGE.

God is a God of changes; which come into us by his Spirit. God is the source of my increase. You cannot trust yourself to stay away from the curse. Jesus puts a strong anointing on us. Things do not work unless God puts His anointing on it. Change your thinking and change your life. Let GOD be GOD. It is important right now that the people of God come together. There are boundaries in the word of God. You have to set boundaries in your life. Stay inside the borders of God's word. We are to forgive our enemies. Put your enemies in our Savior hands. Do what the word says. Different people need different things. Everybody is different. Fence around the house for the privacy. Jesus helped those who came to Him, He did not go saving people. You cannot let people use you, we are to make sacrifices. We do not always make the best decisions. Help people from a distances, no more one sided help in my life.

Everybody is trying many different kind of ways to get money, but one thing for sure God knows your scheme, and where you are. Lack is a disease, and I will not continue to travel with the wrong trendsetters. No one knows how powerful they are until Jesus lights their candle. Darkness creates the path to wrong timing.

I have tried so many different ways to get money, I have sold drugs, stole, gambled and have had the sex just to gain money. Now I know which way is the right way because I have changed my mind about who I will serve. Finally, I can depend on my miracle money and inheritance that God has waiting for me.

After all these years; it is my time! My Heavenly Father told me there is a time for everything under the sun. He will meet my needs according to His riches and glory.

Know When The Spirit Speaks

Most Christians come to church and find their way to another physical need. The enemy will cause you to think he is important. We do not have to be in the boat for him to notice us. You do not have to have a position. Do not be discouraged He just needs to see you there when He gets there. When God gets ready to find people normally he finds people that are already working. Jesus wants to get in the boat, so He can teach the people. He does not want to be too close to them. Even if He did not want to listen He had to. The Lord had to get me in the boat. Do not go too far to quick. Before teaching, you have to be taught. You cannot teach what you do not know. After He finished teaching, He said, *"Launch out into the deep and let down your nets for a catch."* - **LUKE 5:4**.

Get ready to throw your net out there. What is my anchor? Cut the rope. Pull up your anchor. Whatever it is, it has already served its purpose. You cannot do it in shallow water. You are going to get shallow water and you can only get it in deep. Let down your nets. Get ready to work. Use what He gives you. This next assignment is going to be different because Jesus said do it. God will tell you what to do next. Provision comes with provision. Pick a partner not an adversary. Do not call everybody a partner. Know them that labor amongst you as the word says. The boat is bigger than the net. It is a whole lot of fish. Increase is coming. Do not forget to bless the BLESSER. Release into the deep. He is about to tell the people how to bless us.

Chapter Three

Keys

Without money you will not have keys made!" The Lord provided you with powerful keys to open spiritual doors. God gives us keys to the kingdom to bear fruit.

Key to long life:

The only way you can do that is live with GOD. He is the biggest of your needs more than anything else on this earth.

Faith is a key to success:

Do not give up on the Lord's mission. When someone challenges me I need to go above and beyond to excel. I cannot compare my life with anybody else, because what is for me is for me, but I know God has appointed Special Angels to surround and protect me.

Know When The Spirit Speaks

Hebrews 11:1
"Now faith is the substance of things hoped for, the evidence of things not seen."

Happiness is a key to success:
Your heart will determine how happy you want to be. Happiness comes from within. A person can never be happy with what they have because we will always want more. You have to make someone else happy in order to be happy. We have to command what we want and how we should feel in order to live happy.

Word of Knowledge is a gift:
There is nothing I can teach you if you are not willing to know. Open this book again and again for; which I give is a gift. Try to practice the value of knowledge. Showing your imagination is the gateway to knowledge. Never confuse knowledge with wisdom. One helps you survive, the other one helps you live your life. Imagine how important it is to live with knowledge and power. It is better to reveal knowledge than to show ignorance. Let your faith flow with knowledge from your heart, beyond your proof.

ECCLESSSIATES 7:12
" For wisdom is a defense as money is a defense, But the excellence of knowledge is that wisdom gives life to those who have it. "

Obedience is a major key:
From now on I will obey the Lord and His laws. I will carry them out in detail. For the Lord thy God hath blessed thee in all the works of thy hand: He knoweth thy walking through this great wilderness.

Peace on earth is the gift to us from God:
The key to receiving peace is to not worry about things, but pray instead. Peace helps you to arrive and meet your goal. You cannot let outside circumstances affect your mind. Peace comes from love. We all appear and disappear. Everything is changeable. We need an understanding of brunet peace. You have to give peace a chance. Now it is time for us to forgive each other that is the only way we can live in peace and have a peace. You cannot make money and make noise.

WORSHIP IS A KEY:

Reverence for a sacred object; high esteem or devotion for a person; worship releases provision. You have to get worship in order. Flesh cannot worship. Worship is our weapon. Other gifts are waiting.

HAGGAI 2:9

"The glory of this latter temple shall be greater than the former', says the LORD of host. 'And in this place I will give peace', says the LORD of hosts."

Now... What will you do with your keys?

_____
_____
_____
_____
_____
_____

I have the KEYS TO THE KINGDOM!

Ezekiel 12:28

"Therefore say to them, 'Thus says the Lord God: None of my words will be postponed any more, but the word which I speak will be done," says the Lord.

I will not boast about myself it is time to Let Go and Let GOD perform His word. Give God the opportunity to show you. When He closes the door He is the only one that can open it.

The Cleaning Business God let me run is prospering through His grace and mercy! Some fruit was bad and some was good. "Without FAITH it is impossible to be cleansed." The business is for his glory. It was a way of telling me that I had to clean my life up! Thank You Lord You do not know how much this means to me. I never thought I would have made it. If God is for me who cares if anyone else is against me. He has sent me to help the prisoners that are stuck in bondage to proclaim the good news all about Jesus.

Father, I can say that you have really had my back because I told you to take this business away and You actually did it. I say that because I have not been able to manage the finances the way they are supposed to be handled, was over staffed, and employees were not capable of getting the job done when I was not there. It was a learning experience for me. I didn't pay all my debt, but I know you will bring me through the tribulation, and persecution out to rich fulfillment. When you fully give it back; I will know how to run the business and be responsible and wise no matter what happens. God is good, in spite of the situation that I caused. He still has been faithful, supplying my needs, working without business Insurance and that is how I know You are so great and awesome. You have given me another chance because I have it now.

EXODUS 23:25

"So you shall serve the LORD your God, and He will bless your bread and your water, And I will take sickness away from the mist of you."

I am so glad to be alive right now. Be careful of where the Dog lay is Bone! You can catch disease, but you cannot catch health. There's a dangerous dilemma in this Community HIV/AIDS is more devastating of matter. We got to wake- up. Temptation is everywhere, temptation is to try to block the sin out of your mind. Whatever you touch you remember. Do not let the enemy take over. Guard your community. Do not substitute. Be able to say no, when you need to. Jesus went into His flesh... Get the violence out of your mind. Stay in your place. This county we live in, we have more people infected. We need to act like we are married. Be who you are. The Spirit of GOD is not obligated to my flesh. The most productive is Spirit to Spirit. These are things that I have learned. Jesus died according to the purposes of Divine Plans; not to the whims of cowardly people. Just as you and I will die, not according to the taste of cancer, not according to the will of an sinful drunk cruising down along the highway, not according to the will of a painful disease. We will die under the good hand of GOD's private care. We will pass through the valley according to God's clock, not the time table of random fate; IN THE NAME OF JESUS!

JEREMIAH 30:17

For I will restore health to you and heal you of your wounds , says the LORD, 'Because they called you an outcast saying: "This is Zion; No one seeks her."

God is looking to bring some manifestations to the earth. Do not be caught off guard by the distractions. The craziness is going up because of the teachings, catch the things He is speaking right now. This is very serious what God is calling us to. I am valuable and necessary to this movement for the kingdom. Every week we need to be accomplishing something for the Kingdom. God is well pleased with us. We have to re-learn church. God is looking for natural and normal where MEN and WOMEN are married and wake - up together. Marriage is not made to make you happy, it is made to make you holy. Two are better than one. We really cannot change the world, many of us cannot change ourselves. I have to change me. It is not my job to change anyone. God is the one who changes others, but as I mentioned earlier, I choose to be an example for the next generation; to fulfill the promises of God, grace is needed every day.

If there is information; read and understand it. If there are laws; abide by them. If there is a promise, search to find and trust it.

1ˢᵗ THESSALONIANS 4:11-12

"Make it your ambition to lead a quiet life, to mind your own business, and to work with your hands, just as we told you, so that your own daily life may win the respect of outsiders. So that you will not be dependent on anybody."

Chapter Four

Tools for Winning

"Seek ye first the kingdom of God and his righteousness, and all these things shall be added to you" - ***MATTHEWS 6:33***

Repent from selfish thinking. Be obedient. Love the Lord. Pay your tithes and offerings. Ministry is serving. We are to be about the business of serving people. Our serving of them must be the serving of the Lord Jesus Christ. We have to serve The Lord and stop observing. The heart is what we are supposed to serve God with. This is how we do it. Our Heavenly Father wants Kingdom ministry.

Assignment
Read the gospels and focus on the way Jesus did ministry. *******READ IT! ******

I have ministry in me! Most believers do not like hearing that they have a ministry. The interesting thing about that is; pastors want people to serve. God has never called His believers to seek His ministry easy. We do not know what to do. We never know how to become a story. We have to know what to do in our Matron - assigned territory.

The Greek word Matron mean: *a portioned off measure a determined extend a measure or limit.*

We must be transformed by the renewing of our minds. Enough of having confidence you will succeed being yourself. You have to hear God with the inner side of your ear, He is not talking to me from the outside.

The greatest thing we can do is stop murmuring and complaining. What you believe has got to be in your mouth. The spirit of faith is a faith believer living in the word. Abundant grace comes through **THANKSGIVING!** Be ready to train. Giving is the ultimate commitments. I am not going to die now so, stop worrying yourself about me because God got my back!

Do not live in your past. Invest in yourself. Exercise your faith. Be   flexible to God when you move, He moves   just like that.

Pick up your feet.   We have to discipline ourselves. You can be good to someone who was not good to you. You can never look for Jesus where he was. Get in order. Learn to be more mindful. Search for him. Trust God. You have what you need to be a Godly person.

The more we do not stress out about anything the more we learn. You cannot let your feelings run your life. Do not live your life angry. Someday you have to make peace with yourself. We need to let God clean our hearts.

Praise and Worship. Discover what God has said to you.   We need to be doers of the word. Give God a big mouth. Our mouth is holding us back. Watch your vocabulary. You can miss out on God's blessings if you are not obedient to his word. GOD today is still driven to change the world. There are more people out there. Please go and find your lost keys.

Do not ever stop learning, comprehending, and changing. Open up your heart to receive God. We have to guard our hearts and control our thoughts We must educate ourselves. Think about what's ahead of us. Make better decisions. Eat better. Think better. Exercise daily. Drive your business. Make yourself look blessed! Satan does not want us to be blessed. Building something great requires studying what we have already heard; those are the tools. Increase your faith.

As I sat and wondered about how people really are; I realized they can be in the world or in the body of Christ. I realized one minute they are okay with you, then the next they have so much anger built up, and just do not know how to release the pressure. The best way I learned to release is by praising the Lord with all my heart for His goodness and mercy; which endures forever.

You can never find who you really are unless you are in the body of Christ and have on the Full Armor of God. I asked the Lord to give me a Discerning Spirit and use me for His Glory. Some people will never get to see the things I have seen and hear the words I have heard, because of Lack of Knowledge and willingness to yield to the voice of the Lord. I have a calling on my life and am willing to let the Lord use me because Satan had control, but God over powered Him and raised me up so that no weapon formed against me shall prosper. If you take the time and realize that, "He who dwells in the secret place of the Most High shall abide under the shadow of the Almighty God" - **PSALM 91:1.**

I was committing so much war against myself because that was the only way I could relate, but often I think about the past. I now know old things have passed away and my New Beginnings is here waiting to come the pass.............

God had to rearrange some things about me. See; "He has this day set me over the nations and over the kingdom, to root out and pull down, to destroy and to throw down, and to build and to plant" - JEREMIAH 1:10.

God told me:

ISAIAH 1:18-21

"Come now, and let us reason together. Says the Lord though your sins are like scarlet, They shall be white as snow, though they are red like crimson, They shall be as wool, If you are willing and obedient, You shall eat the good of the land, But if you refuse and rebel, You shall be devoured by the sword. For the mouth of the Lord has spoken. Afterward you shall be called the city of righteousness, the Faithful City. "

People everywhere are looking for the Kingdom, even if they do not recognize it by that name. That is why the harvest is for someone to show them the way and the laborers are few. Then the King will say to those on my right,

Mathew 25: 34 - 40

"Come, you who are blessed by My Father; take your inheritance, the kingdom prepared for you since the creation of the world. For I was

hungry and you gave Me something to eat, I was thirsty, and you gave Me something to drink, I was a stranger and you invited Me in, I needed clothes and you clothed Me, I was sick and you looked after Me, I was in prison and you came to visit me," Then the righteous will answer Him. "Lord, when did we see You hungry and feed You, or thirsty and give You something to drink? When did we see You a stranger and invite You in, or needed clothes and clothe You? When did we see You sick or in prison and go to visit You?" The King will reply, "I tell you the truth, whatever you did for one of the least of these brothers of Mine, you did for me. "

Relax your mind, get the proper rest. Everybody is not in your life for a long time, there are folks who are seasonal. If you keep a seasonal friend, the more you produce, if your heart is right. Thank You for the Favor. It was His will to get me involve in His business, but it was my will to tell Him Thank You. Sin can only go for so long. God will pull your covenant when too much sin is involved, those who hear from God. Some of you do not have jobs and you are already Blessed. Be careful who you are around. We always need to be in the right relationship. We were created to be related. The most important relationship in our lives is the one we have with God.

You have to have your own personal relationship with God. When we get in the right relationship with Him then the relationship with everybody else is going to build- up. It will help us deal with the distractions that bring confusion in our lives that tries to destroy our belief. We are made for relationships. We can chose how we participant in a relationship. I LOVE YOU is optional. I KNOW I NEED YOU IN MY LIFE is provisional. Destiny is relation. Relationships are necessary.

I cannot control the people I am related to and everyone is born with a destiny. It is on nobody, but us to understand our calling. "Importance of the relationships!"

Learn how to establish a relationship. It:
Must grow.
Must improve.
Must be fortified.

Know When The Spirit Speaks

Communicate with your hope. Time is what makes a relationship good. Your faith is what delivers Supernatural Post Master. God is not talking, to me to make good conversation with someone else. I know my God has made a way for me. Men will reject you, but GOD will accept you.

Free your mind from frustration and receive manifestations of Power and Wealth. People will forget what I said and people will forget what I did, but people will never forget how I made them feel. It has been really hard for me and my household this year because of the sin that had crept back into my life, but I can change that and will change from my fleshly desires. Doing that is to cast my cares on Jesus and live holy (Block it from my mind).

You cannot run away every time that you have a problem. You have to sit down and talk it out. If you want to get ahead in life; you need someone who is patient and willing to struggle through problems. I want to do what God created me to do. Give your best to your life, great effort, get plenty of energy, and go the extra mile. For all my life experiences it was a little interruption; just to get me closer to my Everlasting King.

"Love is a gift."
I know God LOVES ME.

God is Love and a God of order.

Most important of all; GOD loves you. Stop forgetting the promises in our GOD. Speak love so everyone can hear. It slowly breaks you. Father, knowing you are in love with me is the greatest gift of all. Everyone Loves surprises. A surprise of being surprised is something that grasps your attention. Why does God allow us to have trials in our lives? He wants us to Love him.

How do you know you love Him?

1) Knowing God.
2) Keeping His commandments. All love begins there.
3) Expectations- Our responsibility is the knowing and keeping His laws, and it is accomplished.
4) You have to demonstrate it, communicate it, transfer it, and give it.

5) Do not miss your development, stay sensitive to God.

STUDY

1 JOHN 4:18-19

"There is no fear in love. But perfect love drives out fear, because fear has to do with punishment. The one who fears is not made perfect in love. We love because he first loved us."

God is never surprised, He has all our problems solved before we get them. He knows all things. Gifting is a reward. God is fully in Love with his people. The greatest commandment is to Love the Lord.

DEUTERONOMY 6:5

"You shall love the LORD your God with all your heart, with all your soul, and with all your strength."

JOHN 3:16

"For God so loved the world that He gave His only begotten Son, that whoever believes in Him should not perish but have everlasting life."

You have to love God first, next yourself then others most of all. Love comes when

you are fully committed to God's plan.
Jesus wants to make you beautiful like I am
within. Then that is when others draw to
love you. It will never compare to God's
love toward us. No one can ever love as
deep as he does. It feels good when you
know someone loves and cares for you. If
you do not love God's word you do not
love GOD.

Keep on showing love among yourselves.
We have to overcome evil with good. Love
being the armor of light. The greatest man
from above made people to like me. I am
a LOVER. When I do for people who do
not LOVE me, like JESUS. It is amazing,
extraordinary and goes far beyond the
measurement of my great expectations!

Love wants to give. Love does good things
for people. Love can be felt and seen. Love
people by being understanding. Love is a
beautiful thing. LOVE requires some kind
of action, love will always cost you
something. Be careful of people that you
love to much because they can make you
lose some stuff; which can side track us. If
God is Love, why do we find all this evil

to destroy ourselves? Can you love others when they do not love back? Turn your heart.

The Keys of Love

Love is the key to ANSWERED PRAYERS
Love is MERCIFUL
Love is POWERFUL
Love is   ACTION
Love is KIND
LOVE IS UNCONDITIONAL
Love is COSTLY
Love feels GOOD
Love is PATIENT
Love is PERFECTION
Love can HURT
Love is COMPASSION
Love is SWEET
Love never ENDS

Love is the master key that opens. **Family** is where the LOVE begins. There is Only One Happiness to LOVE and To Be LOVED. Love life and expect your harvest. We must have keys to the kingdom to bear fruit, and they must be given by God.

Know When The Spirit Speaks

MATTHEW 5:44

"But I say to you, love your enemies, bless those who curse you, do good to those who hate you, and pray for those who spitefully use you and persecute you."

Since God is love if we are not walking in love surely people can realize it. If we LOVE God, it will flow through us. Let your love be sincere. If you ever get a great relationship with yourself you can love others. Where I have to start is where I find myself. If you start wherever you are, find yourself and what you are after will come to you. I have already started. God my Life revolves around you to create glory for you forever and ever and teach others your word. Dance and Worship to touch someone's broken spirit. Minister to Nations. Dance represents God's presence, so release your worship by what you are called to do. Also greet and hug. I decree and declare my touches will heal a group of people. I am waiting on God to move me to my next level in Him. The eyes of the world are watching us. You want to be in High Traffic Land. Eyes have not seen and ears have not heard, because if I make a move it probably will not be a great choice.

My hands are anointed and has healing power from the most high God; and He is calling me to come up higher. Your hands can also be dead if you do not us them properly.

We need to be consistent, persistent, and resistant in life construction to maintain your daily walk with Our King. Understand your capabilities and research to know God for you. Learn to establish a relationship with you.

Respond or response - How I respond to God, to others and myself is going to determine my life. The words, thoughts, and deeds are all stimulators. This is the assignment that needs to be put into right alignment before you reach your destiny. We must labor with the Lord in order to prosper. In his word He said rise early, and sit up late because the fruit of the womb is a reward. I am waiting on God right now to see the wonderful miracles that is about to take place at any time. Marriage is one of them along with a child. Keep your eye on the big picture. Who would want to be left behind?

II CHRONICLES 6:9

"Nevertheless you should not build the temple, but your son who will come from your body, he shall build the temple for My name."

II CORINTHANS 8:10

"And in this I give advices, It is to your advantage not only to be doing what you began and were desiring to do a year ago."

So many things I wanted to do a year ago will soon come together for the Kingdom of God. This year; 2015, was new beginning, specifically the month of March and April it has been different and almost unexplainable. I cannot sit around and mope about the things I lost on account of sin. I come back to take what belongs to me and I want it all back.

Do not fall in love with drugs, alcohol, gambling, or other addictive problems. It can take your energy so there is not time to do anything else.

Ecclesiastes 9:10 - HCSB

"Whatever your hands finds to do, do with [all] your Strength."

Know When The Spirit Speaks

Working with people, things will get messy. Everything matters in this season. We have to agree in the process. Let God deal with them and do not worry about their actions. The church is in a season of chaos. Do not let your passion become division.

Passion- is a natural stream of response. Make it apart of all you do. Do not be afraid of the work. Put your hands in the basket and give it time to flourish. The word is the watering. It takes will power. It will take a controlled mind to develop patience. Behavior comes from thinking. Do not give up because things can happen suddenly. Look up when you do not know what to do or bend down and pray. Allow God to do what He is doing. Whatever you do not do is a problem. Too little or too much of something, may be a problem; however, you do it and do it with all your heart; but not to please others. Do it for the sake of God. Do not complain about what you do for others because it will damage your reward. You have the knowledge to know right from wrong.

I do not live to make you happy; I live from above to be a Blessing ... God is still in the Blessing business. How can you curse me when I am already blessed? Nothing, but Love. My Heavenly Father is erasing the marks any way He likes. I am coming for what belongs to me with a sword in my hand, dance through worship, and praise in my mouth to proclaim what to talk about.

I must not deactivate just because you have the user name and password. Let go! If you find the pieces to my puzzle, I will not be mad. He knows. Blessings are not meant to be unselfish with. He loves me through my past. You know why because my future is yet to come. Do not despise me, keep on, and fall back. Do not hold to my issues because you did not form me or birth me and probably did not even bless me. Ask yourself why. God is my fear. Man or woman can do nothing. Things can change at the blink of an eye. I still smile. I do not pull covers. I am trying to be a model for Destiny on the front page of a magazine. I pull down the strongholds because I know what is real; which will keep you talking!

Chapter Five

Prepare To Win

We have to get engaged, involved, and get ready for the fight. The fight has already been won; we are walking it out. Everybody has to be prepared and ready to do their part. I am a soldier.

What is a Soldier?

One who has the gift to conquer anything that comes against them...

Spend a few minutes to describe your meaning:

_____

_____

_____

_____

_____

_____

_____

_____

_____

_____

Each and everyone have a role to play. We are soldiers in the army for the war. You are armed well for this fight. **I will win all battles every day. Do not run away from your afflictions. Whatever you are going through, you are going to come out of it. Your tricks will not work, you cannot do me like you use to do them**.

Now is the time for Holy people to rise up. Everything that the enemy is doing right now is a light affliction. Do not look to the right, or to the left, look straight ahead. God wants to bring you out of the situation you are in.

PSALMS 18: 34
"He teaches my hands to make war, so that my arms can bend a bow of bronze."

I am your Cure to the Answer. The devil is after your faith in God. We are fighting for victory. I have already got the victory. I hope that you are ready to do all that God has called you to do. We win in every battle because we are equipped, empowered, and ready! God wants to use you. We must believe what the word of God says. Activate your defensive and offensive warfare to conquer every demonic stronghold that tries to steal your life from winning. We do not have time to waste; we are in a war. We are meeting in small groups on Tuesday nights for 90 days of the HIM possible, in the houses for citizens of New Birth - Charlotte. Now we are preparing to deliver the message to the streets of America; where I began my knowledgeable struggle with life. My heart is still over there, but my mind has left there. I know that God is here today.

Shake the Devil off God has Power. Anything I need to do I can do it. Miracles come In CANS... Quit thinking you cannot. Jesus can empower what you cannot do. We can do whatever we want to do.

PHILIPPIANS 4:13
"I can do all things through Christ who strengthens me."

Know When The Spirit Speaks

God is not looking back on your sin, He is looking forward. The power that God has, we are equipped with. The same power that raised Christ from the dead is also in you. He wants us to trust him. God I will trust you, I do not know what you are going to do or when you are going to do it, but I'll surely wait on it. I will not worry myself about anything anymore. You have all power on Earth and Heaven. I have forgiven myself for all the wrong choices I have made. From this day onward, I will live the best way I can, so that I can die with no regrets.

You have to believe that you have the victory. That Jesus died for our sins. Your sins are forgiven. You have been born again. You are the light of the world. Get some place where you can get fed the word of life. Believe you are a creation of Christ. I am expected to be aggravated. Do not focus so much on your problem; think about the solution. We need to remain Godly regardless of the situation. We are in transition right now; sent out in our thinking, building us, so we will be able to go places.

LUKE 11:21

"When a strong man, fully armed, guards his own palace, his goods are in peace."

The gift of GOOD-BYE - This is for all the folks that walked out! Thank You, for leaving me. If you had not of left, I would not have got to the point where God wanted me to be.

This will not be the first time I have been by myself. God is doing some BIGGER things than I can see. Stuff is getting ready to come together. Check your seasons. Seasons bring us to a point of change. You cannot get by, you must wait for your time. When nobody else would talk to me; my Jehovah never left me. I can make it through as long as I know His hand is on me.

2 CORINTHIANS 10:3-6

"For though we walk in the flesh, we do not war after the flesh: For the weapons of our warfare are not carnal but mighty through the pulling down the strongholds; casting down imaginations, and every high thing that exalted itself against the knowledge of God, and bringing into captivity every thought to the obedience of Christ; and having in a readiness

*to revenge all disobedience, when your
obedience, is fulfilled."*

Know that GOD has not forsaken you.

Let by GONES be BYE gone!!! I am still
pushing, striving, and building my life for
the better. Praise God for His goodness and
His deliverance. You have to be built up
in prayer and command your morning. It
is no limits to it when you know how
to pray. The results of that is the book of
Acts. Get tapped into the power. There are
a lot of people that do not want to see you
go. You need to find some people that
are going to fight for you. Prayer builds
you up. Men ought to pray and teach your
family to pray. We must go through
tribulation to enter the kingdom of God.
We were born to deal with tribulation.

ROMANS 5:3-5

*"And not only that, but we also glory in
tribulations, knowing that tribulation produces
perseverance; and perseverance, character; and
character, hope. Now hope does not disappoint,
because the love of God has been poured out
in our hearts by the Holy Spirit who was given
to us."*

God is unlimited, so take the limits off of God. Discover your ministry. We are never going to discover our ministry, until we discover our ministry of Jesus Christ. I am a Full-time ministry for God. Ask God to give you the power to free your mind? Allow God to be glorified. Live by faith, not by fear. Fear can hurt your stomach because when it sits, it begin to stink, if it is left in your belly to long. It is best to open your mouth to let out your hurt and pain that has been closed up for quite some time.

Low self-esteem is a big problem for some people who have made a bad choice in life, been neglected, or battled. Satan tries to hold you locked up. God is the one who can heal and release those painful complications. My burden was FEAR; not going with the plan. Giving up before performing, I realized that I am a secret weapon in the hand of GOD. Sometimes you have to press your praise and worship. Form and fashion should not be a worry for us. Fear and every time we face our fears; we gain strength, courage, and confidence. Fear of failure must never be a reason not to try something. The confidence within me is the confidence to achieve, to progress, to comprehend and to accomplish.

The people you associate yourself with will sometimes fear your presents. Always do what you are afraid to do. You block your dreams and blessings when you allow your fear to grow bigger than faith. "STEP OUT ON FAITH!" Fear can keep us up all night long, but FAITH makes one fine move of God.

There is nothing in life that should be feared, except your Father in Heaven. It should only be understood because fears are nothing but a state of mind. People go to greater lengths to avoid what they fear then obtain their desire. The more you fear, the more you have to fear. Be strong and do not fear. You can regret but you are never forgetting.

Are you called to minister to the needs of people and to educate them? Unity must be tight. We do have authority over the devil. Lacking knowledge cause problems. Therefore remember this:

1) Satan is a liar
2) He is a destroyer
3) He is a controller and does not want you out
4) He is the accuser
5) He doesn't like the word
6) He hates a worship-per

Satan comes to steal, kill, and destroy. You have every right to live healed. Fear opens the door for Satan. He uses your feelings, David was a man who spoke about his feelings, and was a master mentor. Satan never showed up until Adam and Eve showed up. You <u>can</u> help what you do. Never let anyone curse your life! Blessings displace curses.

PSALM 112:1

*"**PRAISE** the LORD! Blessed is the man who fears the LORD, who delights greatly in His commandments."*

Christ loves conditions and He lives through me. Life is hard, but God is good. The Lord will lift you up and out of many difficult situations. Jesus will heal you from any disease. Words will change you. Satan shows up through word and music. Do not limit your thinking or plans because who you hang around determines your motives. Find positive people who talk about their need for Jesus. Do not hang around people that are always talking about one another because they can change your way of living for our Heavenly Father. It could be a minor setback until you realize the wrong mind has to be changed.

You have to line up with the word of God. If not, you can make the wrong decisions and let Satan come into your life and lead you somewhere you never wanted to be. You can be pulled away from your mission when people see how good you are doing with your new life, with God in Christ. They will try to hinder you as much as possible if you let them in your life.

You have to have faith and get your mind set on the things that will advance your way of living and thinking. High expectations are within your heart, but you got to let go of some of the people that are contaminating your mind with this foolish appetite, that they have; "Be ye changed and transformed." God will bring you up and out when He sees your praise, and commitment toward His will. If you do not get in the Bible you will not know that healing is waiting for you. Jesus wants to heal you.

LAMENTATIONS 3:25
"The Lord is good to who wait for Him."

If you do not know God loves you, you can miss your healing, He has for your life. You do not want to live under the curse. Every sickness and disease is under the curse. Jesus redeemed us from under the curse.

HOSEA 4:6
"My people are destroyed for lack of knowledge. Because you have rejected knowledge, I also will reject you from being priest for me; because you have forgotten the law of your God, I also will forget your children."

Know When The Spirit Speaks

People will under estimate you, if you let them, and put you in the category of themselves. You can pick and choose your habits; either good or bad. Most of all, people cannot put your past or their past behind because they have not excepted the PASS! We all are imperfect, we have to except some things about a person that we cannot change about them. Also, we have to practice forgiveness. It is a now recession, but I am living in the blessings.

We cannot live like the world even though we have two worlds. One is visible and the other one is invisible. You must follow the word. Take control of your life. If you feel you are been pushed down, get back up and try again. Hold your hand out and feel the pull, and know that you can bounce at any time. Pat yourself on the back, that lets you know how great of a job you have done. Do not get discouraged when folks seem to judge you, push a little harder, it will not hurt. When it really makes you feel good, they will not understand.

Know When The Spirit Speaks

All we ever hear about is the evil; not the good things about a person. Open your mouth to speak out those things. People always try to pull you down with disturbing messages. God's words are the Good News. They seem to talk about everything they possibly can, but will not spread the gospel of Jesus. I got good news finally! I cannot stop talking about Him. You must celebrate and hope that our Jehovah is close to you each moment that you are here. Step into the reign, with the blessings of the good Lord. All my days are better than before.

DEUTERONOMY 26:18

"Also today the LORD has proclaimed you to be His special people, just as He promised you, that you should keep all His commandments"

Today was very courageous, I had to speak blessings into my dear friends life and ask for forgiveness, because the word of God say speak good over everything and every person. You have to turn it up for the LORD and speak positive in the atmosphere. Our minds can lose, if you are not working the plan, the Lord has establish and ordered for you. No one can determine how high or how far you run this race. You make your own choices, and use God's tools to accomplish every battle. Just as the Doctor gives us orders, Our Jehovah - Rapha orders go far beyond and is exceedingly necessary.

Why waste your time and get further behind with the mission and real qualities of life for broken dreams. My daily mission is to be available to meet the need of someone else. Do not waste your spiritual energy on something that is not going anywhere. Learn how to function by using your spiritual blood in your body. Do not get cast away by the evil spirits around you. Little things matter. Follow the word not the world, no matter what. God, please help me to be more successful and to be a mother of genuine confidence, plus a good wife when the time comes.

You know it gets really bad when you cannot depend on your own family to support or help you get ahead in life. It is either the one or the other. They rather see someone else succeed other than the one who grew up in the house with them.

Know When The Spirit Speaks

You never know how much people claim they love you, until you have a gift to offer and they simply by-pass you and go to the next person that they do not even know. Help others and others help you. I am not mad; but I am just speaking on how I feel. Life goes on.

We have so many paths that we try to take to fulfill our dreams. Paths of fame, fortune, joyfulness and power. It takes us into deeper mire. We are trapped thinking that is our only way out. This pain needs to be cured. It only leads further down to the pit. If not soothed, with the right formulas. Everyone needs to be directed and have models to follow for perspective purpose. So much knowledge thoughts in our heads are filled with, but souls are empty and spirits are so low.

A lot of wasted values. Most people have lost their drive because of unfulfilled dreams. You must be filled with the Holy Spirit of God to refocus life's journey. Emptiness comes when your life draws apart; away from God. He only makes us complete and full. Time does not wait on any man. Stop taking these false paths and settling for nothing. Time is running out. Do not be deceived any longer. Satan was designed to crush, and crumble your work. We have been plagued and troubled with the same problems. The curse of sin. The only remedy is Christ anything else will not work.

Stop putting new labels on these same old bodies. The results of sin are still the same thing. It still leads to death; no matter how you try to figure it out. You cannot escape, you will experience it. Be constructive enough to know your channel or when to turn in this generation. Sit down and recognize when God speaks to you; different timing, but the same message. See your way out of these broken stones by reading this guide and abiding in truth to find wisdom. We are the ones who need correction. If only I can change a few it would make a difference. I really want attitudes to change and children to respect their parents, elders, teachers, and know their rights plus values and diseases to be healed. Those were my struggles so I work on it forever, no more will I ever worry about another person's business. It has been talked about, so all I can do is kneel about it and live out God's laws. Also I need to be ready when He comes back for me.

Man will show you false promises. God's promises are rich and meaningful, filling for the missing pieces, life, treasures, Colors of jewel brilliance. Silver, gold, purple, diamonds, and pearls. In glamorous lifestyle if chosen; everybody does not know who God is. They do not know He is: forgiving, loving, caring, spiritual, able to chastise and corrects you, unchangeable, and will be there when you call on Him.

Some think He does not even exist; while others know how wonderful He is. It is amazing how we meet Him through trials and tribulation. He is the creator of the universe. Creation was manifested through Him. He is in charge of Heaven and Earth and governs everything from the beginning to the end. In order to know Him: you must get saved, pick up the Bible, read and maintain His commandments carefully.

Know When The Spirit Speaks

Do not be fooled by these other gods who leave you hopeless, diseased, disappointed, mind incarcerated, and limited. He is immeasurable, and is not limited to boundaries. Most of all He can see you when you do not even see him. We focus so much on what can be seen; not knowing what is ahead. He is the only one that keeps the stars in place, clouds in the sky, sun beaming, winds blowing, seasons rolling, rain pouring, and miracles coming. Do not put limits on Him.

He is a Spirit that makes things happen and come to pass. You must understand Him. He corrects you when needed. Furthermore, God is Holy, righteous, pure, without flaw or blemish; full of light. He was the only one to bear the sins of the world. His only begotten son was sent to reach Him. He does not hear our cry if we ignore the help. He was sent for our mercy, but the sin we commit separates us from GOD. You have to try Him for yourself. God did what He needed to do for His completed task. Now He gives us the freedom of making choices, right or wrong. Just know the heart of your problem.

Chapter Six
Road to Success

GENESIS 24:12
"Then he said, "O LORD God of my master Abraham, please give me success this day, and show kindness to my master Abraham."

No matter what road you travel, nothing can stop you from making it to your destination, if your determination is stronger than your motivation. God never shuts one door without opening another. You may get a flat tire, you may come up against many obstacles, but if your determination is so strong that nothing on that road you come up against will stop you from making it to your destination, anything and everything is possible through Christ who strengthens you. The road to success may be a struggle, but it is definitely a learning experience. So stay positive and surround yourself with positive people. Being positive will guide you to success. Keep insurance because you might just have a wreck and if you are not insured; that can be a problem.

Take your gear out of park and put it in drive. Make sure you wear a seat belt because this road comes with a manual and it sometimes requires maintenance. When you put your feet on the accelerator; that means go. You do need to use signals if you have not made it to your destination. The Lord has put you in your own lane. Why turn if your life is not right. The Lord can take you on a totally different route, just be prepared for the change of directions, pay close attention to the instructions. Prioritize the way.

How does it feel to be going down a road you never been down before, but you know there is something ahead of you. If you go over the speed limit, you might just get a ticket, so check your speed. Transportation is very important if you are traveling down the road to success. No need to check your rear view mirror because what is behind me does not matter. Why try to stop, what cannot be stopped. Keep your windows earnestly rolled up so you will not be misled, by all the negative sounds of society. Turn the AC on and relax cause it is going to be a bumpy ride down the road to success. Make sure your windshield wipers work because it may rain, but not to worry, cause rain is considered "Blessings."

You may get homesick, but those are feelings that you have. You may get hungry along the way, but thank God for whoever invented the drive-thru. Also, you can take His word and eat it and keep it moving because that is all you'll need to survive for you to succeed.

Success without honor is an unseasoned dish. It will satisfy your hunger, but it will not taste good because the two hardest things to handle in life are failure and success. Pray that success will not come any faster than you can endure. Now do you really feel that the road to success is challenging? (I do because it is considered to be given a salary.) There is only one success to be able to live your life, according to the Kingdom way. Now do you achieve success? Well for one thing you do not define it before you achieve it.

JOB 21: 29

"Have you never questioned those who travel?
Have you paid no regard to their accounts?"

Success is simply not a matter of luck it's favor or failure. There is no success like your own success. It means getting what you want. Happiness wants what you get. Success and failure, we may look at them as being opposite, they are really not because they are companions. The hero and the side kick. It seems to be more of a matter of hanging on after others have let go. The closer a person gets to the top, the more a person finds out there is no top. So judge your success by what you had to give up, in order to get it because success has made failures out of many men or women. I can not wait on success, so I won't be left out or without.

Sometimes I worry about being successful in a mediocre world. I might as well take a nap because the road to success is where ever people need another road. Success is not a desire it is a promise and it is a choice that has to be made. That could be God trying to slow you down. Pay close attention to your signs. There are many directions you can go down this road to success. Our God will give you traveling mercy, and frequent flyers mileage.

ADT called me about an alarm system today. Alarms warn you from someone coming into your surroundings, to invade your property. Always secure and protect what belongs to you. God says He will protect you with his angels, and His up righteous hand when you follow His will. Thank You Lord for signs, wonders, and miracles. Remember we have to reach our destination at all times. Our mighty King is the biggest of our need more than anything on this earth. Watch out for new routes, traffic was backed-up on I-40, so the Lord directed us to a total different route back home which was 15/501= 0.0299 24/27 with the navigation system. Prepare for detours. Take your time. I play by the rules. It took us on a route pass Troy, NC.

Know When The Spirit Speaks

He will make an easier way than I would. It is not what you have in your life, it is about who you have with you. It is all up to your destination, the way you get lead and the side of town you live on makes a difference. You got to pass water if you are traveling on this road to success. You have to be a Walking Miracle. I drove pass water each time that I got on the road to travel, so now I have a swimming pool in the back yard, which was in His plans because I wrote the vision as directed. God has specifically chosen your blessings and curses according to your obedience.

I Got on the highway stopped at Bojangle's in Salisbury located at 985 Peeler Road. I had to use the restroom, so I decided to buy a lottery ticket. I played four different numbers. One was 321 and placed them on the dashboard on May 18th. I did not check them until May 20th, but on May 19th, the number came out. Someone picked up my ticket and they was not even supposed to put her hands on anything that does not belong to her. That is how blessings get messed up; by putting your hands on other people belongings. Keep your hands to yourself. I have learned to keep my hands to myself and off other people's belongings.

ECCLESIATES 10:10

"If the ax is dull, and one does not sharpen the edges, then he must use more strength; but wisdom brings success"

Pay attention when the Bible gives you directions. People can be a hindrance to me from getting my blessing. Where God is going to take you in your life, everybody cannot go because of their faith. Your future to your life is not dead, it is just sleeping. Worship is going to start with the leaders; then the church. Most people are coming in trust. We need to touch Jesus so He can touch them and all the people shall shout with a loud voice.

Chapter Seven

Regrets

Things I have done that make me regret are: having sex before marriage and it being unprotected. Many of us put two people between ourselves. We regret for the past and for the future. I have some regrets in my life. I think all things happen to us for a reason. The things we face helps build character; which molds and make you a much better person. We all must suffer some regrets and pain due to not listening and carrying out God's perfect instructions. Some may have missed the open door because of looking at the closed door for so long. You may get left behind if you are not willing to go forward. Procrastination usually will hold you back. We should do things at the proper time instead of putting things off. It took me

89

some time to realize who I AM and what I had inside of me, that had to come out. Oh, how great and awesome it feels to be able to share what has been held back for so many years. It is a release. I wrestled and struggle for this to come forth, but it was up to God to bring it to the fore front. This feeling is so overwhelming, but I had to wait on Jesus, and also had to walk with him daily to receive my inheritance.

JOSHUA 1:6

"Be strong and good courage, for to this people you shall divide as an inheritance the land which I swore to their fathers to give them."

My biggest regret in life is that I waited so long to serve the LORD, but I thank my God that I still have breath to Bless His holy name.

Disappointments can lead to regrets. I hate being disappointed. The way you handle disappointments will determine your success and grant your heart desires. It can scar you if you are not mature. I hope that you become extremely successful in lieu of your disappointments. You have to expect greater things to be created for you. Opportunity is everywhere, and it is like reaching for something that is so close by. You have to reach at all times in life today.

The more I talk about it; the enemy wants to slow me down, when I needs to be writing about it. The story must be told.

Never mix Business and pleasure because the person who you are in a relationship with does not respect you or appreciate you. Do not let them know how much you are making. On both ends money can get confused. They feel like their job is not important as the owner when in relationship. Make sure you hire people that can go do the job without your presence. Sin is in the word business.

It does not matter who would take me out because God will bring me out anytime of the day. He is not ashamed of me, He loves me regardless of all my flaws and reputation. My God told me wherever I go He will be with me and make my way prosperous, and I would have good success. Something we need the most; we often turn away from it, "LOOKING BACK," I put regrets behind me so I can stay focus on what is ahead of me.

We must solve our own life circumstances and be responsible and accountable for ourselves. Why not rebuild your life no matter what you have been through. When we have the power to making wise decisions. You have to want to change your situation and decide to make the right choices. Everyone looks at the outside, but does not know what is on the inside of a person. Take care of the inside. You have to LET your past experiences go because you could carry it on and clutter, will continue to damage your mind. Every day you wake-up there is something different that needs to be accomplished.

Self- improvement was one of the greatest experiences for me. Life is like putting a blind fold over your eyes, walking down the street. You never know who you are passing by, so be careful and listen to the voice inside of you. We all have blind spots.

That is why we have to take the blinders off to see beyond measurements. The roles people play do no exceed great expectations when the cause is needed. If it is not their dream, it really does not matter to them, but I can succeed because I am willing to go the extra mile for any purpose of my time and life.

We have to learn how to communicate and interact with each other. My past experiences help me to expect a brighter future. All of us have secrets and they must be dealt with. It is not easy bringing them to the table. Dreams are meaningful and some come true. Bad dreams can be transformed to good, if willing to have faith. I have had dreams to come true. Some dreams that I have are dreams to warn me about Heaven and Hell, but I will not give up on my dreams. My dear daughter woke-up crying and said to me mother do not leave me she had a dream that I had left her and died and all she could do was hug me and wept. I told her do not cry. I am not leaving you and that I was going to serve our Lord. I then told her do not worry and stop crying; I love you. She does not want to be left alone, but we all have to leave this world one day or another. That is why we are supposed to;

PROVERBS 22:6

"Train up a child in the way he should go, And when he is old he will not depart from it. I am a fighter, and fighters win. But most of all I do not regret this life I chose."

As I continue to succeed, trying to live the way the Lord planned for me to live; many things come through to discourage me. However, God has a special plan, and blueprint for me and no one can take it away, but Him or I. I know Jesus is the center attraction of every part of me. He has fearfully and wonderfully made me. He is sending me out to different places that I thought I would never have entered. Also, He has sat me down in the face of people who I never thought that I would come in contact with.

We should continue to build a kingdom life. No matter what you do it is never enough for man, so continue to do what is right in the sight of Jesus. Ladies we have to let men know that we do not work for them, we are supposed to be their wives or help mate. Stop worrying about other people. Leap forward and express your love to the needy. God notices what needs to be done in the body. Coming up in life I did not get to laugh and express my feelings for anything in the world. I did not get the mother, daughter talks. My mother had so much fear, hurt, and pain; she could not relate with her kids. We only knew rage in her voice.

When not giving the chance to speak and not knowing how to speak; it causes dreams to be annoying. He will reward you every second of the hour. It is not too hard to follow His laws and commandments. As He prepares the way to express yourself graciously to be heard, because trapped pain can kill you quicker than anything else.

Christ commands us to let go of anger, bitterness, hurt, and pain. The pattern is set for us to follow and to live longer than the enemy has tried to set for us. People notice things when they do not get done. Always keep a clear mind to fulfill your vows. Stretch yourself, hold your posture straight , massage your back and neck as often as needed to relieve the pressure points. Things happen for many reasons. Life is full of warnings. You have to learn how to slow down as often as needed, because things run out of your way.

Sometimes other people's problem is a burden on you, but they say bare others burden. Be alert and always play the game the way it is supposed to be played! Get by yourself and think. Set aside time for planning, organizing, and adjusting. Give yourself time to simply experience and enjoy. Give yourself a moment; think Joy. Smile at life, even when life has not smiled at you first. Be the first one to initiate goodness and you will be the first one to benefit from that goodness.

At any given moment, including right now, You are fully deserving of life's greatest experiences. It is never too early and it is never too late as long as you have your breathe. Go forth! We must hear on the inside. Pay attention to what you hear.

Value the word that is preached. It must be protected. We must never stop doing what is right when you know it is right and you do it all over again. You have to be faithful. Your roots have to be holy. There is danger behind every wall and the only way you can defeat danger is with Christ. It may take twelve to fifteen years before you see results with conquering danger. If you do not use your legs for the Lord, He can stop you in your tracks. Your actions speaks inside, follow your dreams, extend yourself and you will be promoted.

It could be whenever and whatever I do, BUT sometimes it does not go the way that I plan. My help comes from the Lord.

Satan thinks that he trapped me, as long as I know I am saved he cannot stop God's glory; that is due back to Him. Understand we are not the only ones that are blessed. When something is broke I know it can be fixed or replaced. No more debates, the devil has revealed himself to me. He tries to continue to make me powerless. Shame on him for bringing my tears. I am bringing everything to God. I am burning and building. It was not easy, but it was worth it. God has released me to advance because I'm so much stronger now.

Stop fighting, touch someone and say no matter what happens never lose heart to seek God. Anytime you are doing good the devil will raise his head. Do not reject the messenger, sometimes He uses other people to minister to you just listen! Have no fear. Do not fight at all. The more you fight the worst it gets. The enemy gains strength through my fighting. Rest and be relaxed.

What you can do is worship. When you worship, it will cause Jesus to come and see what happen or to see about you. Take your war clothes off in the presence of the Lord. After the battle is over will come your harvest; a great blessing. I am glad I am not perfect. Stop eating so you can bring your flesh under subjection. Your flesh prohibits you from hearing. Brag about GOD to GOD. These same enemies are still here trying to fight against me. God knows something about this enemy, you do not know. When you fight, you get more entangle with the cobweb. Let the spider alone.

David had many enemies. He had no problem killing people and had no problem destroying the enemy of God. He chased after God like we chase after foolishness. If the head is blessed, all are blessed; but if the head is cursed the whole house is affected. If the head gets right, everything else will line up. Pray for the head.

Satan has no problem provoking. Pride goes to destroy it. Every leader needs leaders to tell them they are about to make a mistake. Listen to people who have wisdom. If the blind lead the blind, you both will end up in a ditch. The sin I have committed has displeased God, so He had to punish me. God hates sin! Stop sinning. Instead of falling into the hands of man, I would rather fall into the hands of God. What has already happen is causing pain. It is still in effect. If it was over, there would not be any instructions. Get the plaque out of your house, if there is trouble somewhere. It always has signs. Do not live in confusion.

If you leave trouble to long, it begins to affect the norm.

I have a reason to be happy because I am still standing. Speak Lord, my hands are so anointed. My hands, if not using them for what they are called to do, they will perish from uselessness.

You abused your calling. Thank you for smiling down on me. I am going to enjoy who God created me to be. Oh what a wonder, He is. REGARDLESS of the injury that was done to my finger. I am on the loose with my hand on the cross. Stretched out getting ready to do my work. Enjoy what you do! Let God make you what He wants you to become. Equipment is needed so make sure you have what is needed. Experience should come from your lifestyles to impact your spiritual salvation. The best thing I know is that God has no regrets about me.

Chapter Eight

Backtracking

When I go back to the familiar areas it seems as though my spirit connects with the same spirits, but at the same time it keeps me striving to get higher and higher. Watch this tour you can try it; only if you accept the price behind it. Reprove yourself and catch this plane it is about to start. No matter what has happen you cannot catch me, I am on fire. You can find me in the center of greatness; climbing this mountain and aiming my rocket because it is about to explode.

When getting life together, you have to leave people behind to catch this reality that I am living. Everything comes in dreams; never forgotten, but be sure to make the good dreams come to life in order to serve these nations that you must get ready to minister.

Let your true qualities show. You must have a team behind you to shelter your presence. Get ready to drive the devil away from you, while the Lord is with you. I am trying to demonstrate how this life that was planned to be, elevated. Let me remind you, if you had forgotten; doing the same thing, but a different way. God said come as you are, He can work with that. We have to realize that He is waiting on you, you are not waiting on Him. He may not come when you want Him to, but He is always on time. Wait on God's timing and you will not waste your time. Do not give Him your left overs give Him what is right. This lesson comes in parables truthfully waking you up, wherever you may be.

I did not give my body enough time to develop, whether it was in need of nourishment or self-control. I can imagine how many pounds I weighed when I was born. I was underweight since the beginning by the structure of my bones according to the doctor. I know I was full term, but will not complain over the past. I have not seen baby pictures to remind me of the precious beginnings of my life. Which I know I was an adorable looking child. As I grew, I saw no smile at all.

You can find me up in the sky or through a rainbow. I am coming out, my mind is so qualified and highly needed for whatever I put my hands to. I trust the agreement. I had to step out of line to put people in their place so the right people can get in front to lead the way. I got to go! I cannot be late, it can cause you to lose this fight. The dog in me is powerful because I have to be protected from my enemies.

I have to study and show myself approved. Time with God the Father helps you maintain healthy relationships. You may not know it, that is why you are supposed to wait. I am not going to run from any one. I have no fear, but will you ever forgive me? It seems as if it is a chess game. It took me this long to become strong.

Now I cannot get stuck in life because I know Jesus heals. I cannot live in fear.

Nobody talked about the things that happened in their life. They kept it in, because of fear. They would not tell you the consequences not even the real deal about life, because they had been hurt or had their face behind the door. I noticed a lot of people cannot face you when they have done you wrong but do not let it stop you. Deal with your problems. I will not give- up. Everybody is making wishes on wishbones when they need to be praying for a backbone. Be willing to make more sacrifices for the Lord. Just do it; this is your day.

Never give in. I just want to let the world know we serve an awesome God. All power is in heaven. We will experience a release of double abundance and favor this year of 2014 overflowing into 2015. I see the people peeping, waiting for the glory to begin. When you see me, you see heaven kicking in. I know you are doing your job keep it true to the end. God is at the top of greatness.

I will never forget the day, I begin writing, and singing. My friend was in an abusive relationship. Her baby daddy was abusing her. I can relate because I was sexual abused by my male cousins which they had me doing provocative things at a very young age. The man who was supposed to have been my father abused me sexually; which led me to be abusive to others. I became addicted to it and was so diseased. The instructions determine the future you create, but God graced me to overcome. Why live low when you can live a good life. We all have the opportunity to cause greatness to be possible in our lives. Your sin stops you from receiving the blessings.

Keep your covenant which is an agreement with the Lord. The church, God set you in place, please figure your part out. Do not leave with a premature blessing because of allegations against someone. We all have fallen short of his glory. I left the church, but it was not for that reason, it had to be my sin. Be very delightful and diligent according to your purpose, plan, or calling. People leave you because they cannot handle the pressure or situations and do not want to do God's assignment. God gives and forgives; while man gets and forgets.

We shall live, get healed, and not die! Who goes to check me? Time is flying. Who goes to stand? My Farris wheel spinning and cobwebs twisting. Some people wants you to starve, and some people want you to eat, but what I am trying to get you to understand is God wants you to survive. Open up your heart. Do not cover up your pain with what remains from the past and newness will be given to you.

I had to get off track to get it right. The spot light is so very bright when you're trying to get it right. Dealing with people in your past who do not understand, will always remind you of your past. Stay focus on what is ahead. Folks say I need to learn how to talk, but some people need to learn how to stop talking. Sometimes we need to mind our own business. We were not born to be perfect. We were born to be a Blessing.

Know When The Spirit Speaks

When people hurt you keep calling and if you do not get the response you want, do not take it the wrong way. Keep it right. All you can do is ask for forgiveness, it is up to the other person to accept it. Do not have hard feelings towards the person because what they are saying may hurt you, but instead use it to help and motivate you. Still Love them no matter what. No one can take your Love away. That helps you to step up and move forward. You just got promoted to the next level to get it in. Thank You and God bless you. That means you had to put the telephones down and focus more on your next move.

We have made so many things to be our idols; why let the blind lead the blind? The wicked people will always try and find a way to kick you down. I was even told that I was a hypocrite. You know why people can always seem to talk about other people, but when it happens to them they cannot handle reaping what they have sowed. PEACE UNTO YOU I LEAVE!

PSALMS 41:4-7
"O LORD I prayed has mercy on me. Heal me, for I have sinned against you" But my enemies say

nothing but evil about me. "How soon will he die and be forgotten?" They ask.

They visit me as if they are my friends, but all the while they gather gossip, and when they leave, they spread it everywhere.

All who hate me whisper about me, imagining the worst for me. But most important of all he has preserved my life because I am innocent.

I'll dwell in his presence forever. God has anointed me, he's pouring oil of joy on me, more than anyone's else."

Extricate yourself from drama to enjoy your journey. My help comes from the LORD WHO MADE HEAVEN AND EARTH. Smiling in my face trying to take my place, that is how it is, when you do not live for Christ. I have done it so you better think twice before you enter my life! Invade my flow and keep watching my steps. You can peep. I see you looking, your blinds all torn, from you watching. If you want the truth? Open your BIBLE! If you look at my shoes, you can follow my moves, but definitely you cannot walk in them.

Everyone has an addiction; whether saved or unsaved. We all have to find out the problem and seek healing. From crawling, to walking, from sitting down to getting up, from crying to laughing, know yourself before you try to figure out someone else life. We all have to learn how to accomplish this tasty, lustful appetite. You will need to dissect it like you was getting surgery. Examine your disorder. Dismiss or divest the substance and dominate the interior or exterior to discover the damages of the mind. When the mind is mischievous and cloudy it can disrupt your thinking and cause confusion, dispute, dismays, distrust, distress, distraught, distraction, division, divorce, doubtful, down, double-minded, drama, drowsy, and depression; which comes from domestic violence.

All the negative formulas generates through a generational curse that has to be broken. It was passed through the parents. Give positive direction and lead to the best of your ability. I am a Living legend, original who will overcome sickness and danger. Overhaul is the purpose, overall the circumstances. If it takes for me to be in solitary? Lord forbid, that is what I will do to get my mission accomplished.

Satan can attack your well being if you feed your flesh. The price is expensive, and the wisdom is priceless. Specialize and specify your menu and put space between the both of you. Speculation is a bad story to the spirit. Use a strategy board to make history. Never expect the worst. Bountifully bounce the ball in the basket to shoot your greatest shot. Do not rationalize if you miss your point of action or your hour of rank. Ratify, and rotate your position. Roam the role; shelter the victory. Shuffle and shovel the wasted materials that are stuffed inside. Figure out a way to make them come out. Wait until the door is open before entering and make sure the door is shut while exiting, because there is always a surprise behind the doors of life. Watch for the sign of a warrior. When someone shoves you and makes you fall, it normally does not feel good, but look for your promotion. Greater things wait when you get back up. It feels good to be able to put a smile on your face or on someone else. Giggle to show that you are glad. Take all frowns and lay them to the ground. It is not good to be so serious because you can take the joy out of your heart. Others will always think they know your situation. When all these steps are taken, it will bring it into fruition. You will see the fruit of your works. No need to hide your true happiness. Success defines happiness. Furnish the correct tools at all times, because if you look in the dictionary, none of your words would be misspelled. Learn the meaning of your true background.

Shun negative role models completely because they will delete value from your character. Throughout my circle everyone wants to characterize me instead of receiving or recognizing me as a tool. You need to handle me like I am valuable. Always try to placate when you feel that it is needed. I often sit and wonder why is it such a problem when you have a High Calling on your life. We seem to run away and try to hide. Instead we should move along with the calling, and watch the steps. You should be producing fruit abundantly, so that it should remain. It would let you know if your true walk with Jesus is put into effect. Living in sin can cause you rising medical bills, hurt, distractions, late payments, poverty, worry, pain, frustration, loneliness, hindrance, hunger and many more curses. The decision is yours to make. Righteousness produces wonderful feelings. Light produces time of the day, darkness is controlled by the time of night. Do not let sin drive you out of your office. Low living can kill you quicker than a disease because you are living life under too much pressure that will cause sickness. We must sing a new song for restoration. God is gracious. Unstop your ears and listen. Your whereabouts are revealing spiritually. It is good when the Lord calls your name twice and you answer. It is not good to have ears if you do not hear.

Look to be saved for the right purpose, not just for the benefits. Hugs are so expensive; they will exalt you. Be cautious of others touches because their spirit can be unclean and it could rub off on you. Go to God and tell Him, you made a mistake. I have sinned against You and myself, I need to get me and You back, I have learned my lesson.

YOUR EYES TELL THE STORY

Let your love flow. God loves me the way that I am. Learn to appreciate who you are. Nobody knows what the future holds.

People hide behind shades, hoodies, caps, masks, in the back, or even in the dark, so no one will notice who they are, but no need to hide. I notice what others will never know. Locks on phones; you got so much to hide. Stay away from the house to answer your calls. Play games like never before. Codes are being picked. People do not answer phones and act like they do not see the call because what they hide can be found. Stick around long enough the story will be told. If you look into someones eyes you can basically see what they have been and are going through.

ISAIAH 9:2
"The people who walked in darkness have seen a great light; those who dwelt in the land of the shadow of death, upon them a light have shined.

ISAIAH 9: 6
"for unto a child is born, unto us a son is given: and the government shall be upon his shoulder: his

*name be called Wonderful Counselor what they
have been through Mighty God, Everlasting Father,
or done in life. Prince of Peace"*

Thank you for turning on my lights of
darkness. God sent people to teach me His
will. Light is sweet for the eyes. When
people go by so many different names that
were not given to them by their parents,
they normally have something to cover-
up. That lets you know people better than
themselves. Watch the eyes. They say
carrots are supposed to be good for our eyes.
(Eat plenty!) I want to be a more interesting
person. You have to be taught right, when
the time comes. I have changed. I am not
who I used to be. You can reverse from
doing wrong to the right way. You can live
to be who you were supposed to be,
before sin was revealed. The future tries
to warn us. People can think what they
want, I do not care what they think. You
can decide. Life is a mystery. You have to
earn respect and trust. You have to face your
problem. The world did not give me my
joy and the world cannot take it away.
This happy face that I am wearing; Jesus
wants me to wear it for you. He touched my

eyes and nothing else will ever be the same.

I need someone that can reach my heart and not just the top layer. I believe His word, but in the kingdom He would supply my every need. I smiled to God, because He told me man could not satisfy me like He will.

Brokenness begin on my couch at home. Love can be seen in the eyes. I love to see my mother smiling, which I very seldom see. Learn to love; it is easy. Get use to the family of God.

Sinner's eyes are seen in the dark. Step into the water to be cleansed. Let Jesus touch you and fill you with his love. Open your eyes so you may see through these troubled times. All this sin and shame that you are involved in. My new life is waiting.

God gives us different ways of doing things. People think they do not need God. He will always be where you think He is not. We have to function as a team. Do not use your past experiences for your present situations.

Do not hurt others; you have to humble yourself to have peace. My soul is at rest. I give you thanks Lord. I am so blessed.

COLOSSIANS 3:13
"Bearing with one another, and forgiving. One another, if anyone has a complaint against. Another; even as Christ forgave you, so you also must do."

Let your confidence fill your heart with joy. You have to like yourself. I am glad to share this history. I got so much to tell. This is a good memory of great moments. God formed me and He matched me perfectly for you. I did not come here to ask you for anything, I just want to talk and tell you I AM LOVED!

If you are thirsty please drink the living water. God is good not every once and awhile, but He is good all the time. Your King is coming. Open your eyes so you will not miss your time. It is a lot more that is going to be expected of me. My children's wealth is my business. I must publish this message. It is fun to be a writer and be able to write THINGS DOWN THAT NEED TO BE HEARD. Right conditions bring things forth. It is a pleasure to be able to be in the power of human connection. It is good to have people you can count on.

Love is something we do; not something we say. Count on the Lord and count your blessings, recounts are okay. Nothing can keep you from my Love, my child. Our standards are high. Are you prepared? There is no such thing as a nobody. Everybody has a habit to support. Forget what you do not have and praise God for what you do have. It is your season for you to be blessed. We need to find the breaker to bring us out. Hell is no joke; turn to Jesus. Salvation is free, but not until you ask for it. I have learned that dead things will put a curse on you and let the dead bury the dead. Let go of things that impact your righteous decisions and cause you to make wrong decisions. Do not give up because things can happen suddenly. Keep, keep, keeping it up, please do not give up. Each day I walk with Jesus He expands special moments and gives me time to build my destiny to reign. Everything repeats itself. You need to know how to live, and change your heart; Free, freed, and freedom is yours to be but you must seek then you shall find.

ECCLESIASTES 9:11-12

"I returned and saw under the sun that -- The race is not to the swift, nor the battle to the strong, nor bread to the wise, nor riches to men of understanding, nor favor to men of skill; but time and chance happen to them all. For man also does not know his time: Like fish taken in a cruel net, like birds caught in a snare, so the sons of men are snared in an evil time, when it falls suddenly upon them."

Through the eyes of a child of God nothing should be forgotten. When we are empty, You fill us and when we are hungry, You fed us. When we are naked you clothe us. Your soul has to be fed. From God's hand there is no shortage of Love. For the glory of the Father; peoples obedience will be seen. Nations will rejoice to lift up His name.

Look at the sunshine that God brings and the rain, that means He can change anything at any given time. Look at the difference He can make in your life. Let your heart change daily to live accordingly to God laws. You can see that I do not have much, but as long as I have Jesus, He will provide. His blessings are on me. I carry Him everywhere that I go. Freedom is free. Run me Lord because I know I have a home on the other side. My home is in Heaven. He is preparing my way. Stand and enjoy your purpose.

Human eyes can see through the human soul; as if that humans soul is at the end of the road. Dig a little deeper, you may have to be still and know that I am God. He is watching us. Expect something new and receive this fresh anointing. Feel the wind and know something will blow your way. Enter the gateway for your supernatural of God. He will become natural in your life. Emotions can destroy your way of thinking. We have to make some adjustments about self to receive peace. I cannot change the world, but I can change myself by changing my character and ambitious about life. I believe in doing things according to God; not man because I believe His way can manifest through me. Be prepared to act like heroes. Look what I have seen through spiritual eyes.

Know When The Spirit Speaks

Have you ever been through something and did not know what was going on? Even as children of God you have adversaries. Adversary- *is anyone who comes in your life who does not want you to prosper.* My adversary heard some things about me. You did not know you had an adversary until you started working and building. Be on the lookout in hopes that your adversary does not present them self to you. Everybody that likes you is not like you. The Holy Spirit will discern for you. You were frustrated. Frustration is different from being attacked. Frustration- *is a chronic emotional feeling state of insecurity, or dissatisfaction arising from unresolved problems or unfulfilled needs.* Let it die because you are never going to resolve it, but Jesus can. Passion means suffer, but it brings compassion. Look in your life where you suffer the most. You must be willing to wait on your appointed time. While waiting study and read. They have killed, deaden, and made inactive, your spiritual gifts. Stir up your gifts. Reactivate! God is about to use you. You do not want to be so frustrated that you do not receive God.

Chapter Nine

Get Ready To Finish

God does not discriminate against anyone because He loves sinners just as He loves believers. He sat down with saints and sinners both He healed, delivered plus set free. Lay your bad habits down. We must be the ones to win this battle. He created us to succeed when He made us, because He told us to be fruitful, multiply, and subdue the earth.

GALATIANS 3:13

" Christ has redeemed us from the curse of the law, having become a curse for us, for it is written, "Cursed is everyone who hangs on a tree".

You have to work on your relationship and protect your rights. Hang-on to God and never let go of his expectations. I want to do things right. Have you ever been around someone who does not want to see you smiling and happy? Continue to try and make them happy even when they do not know the meaning of joy.

There is a part of me people will not understand. It is natural to accept one another. When being reminded of your past; it hurts. Especially, when you know things could have been discussed a little better than anticipated. I want to be part of the solution instead of the problem.

You always expect me to pick up your pieces. It takes a good woman behind every man to get things done. Sometimes when I react; I am wrong. I am really hiding my talents deep down inside and it does not feel good. Lowering your standards to accommodate someone else is the wrong choice. It affects my well-being: financially, physically, and mentally. This shuts me down from performing my praise dance for the Lord. Let us come together and defeat the traps so we can jump over the hurdles that were there before the both of us. I do not leave time for people to annoy me.

Confirm, agree, control, and be determined through making difficult decisions of what cannot be done. Prove to society that you do not have to give-up. The enemy loves to try and keep us behind in darkness instead of light. Release yourself to climb out of your nest to hatch. Use your Christ ability to come out. No one can stop you. You are the only one who can stop the missionary. Do you believe God can do all things through you?

Explain-

_____
_____
_____
_____
_____
_____
_____
_____
_____.

I cannot depend on myself to go forward I put all my dependency on the one above the heavens. Every time I think of violence

I remember how it caused so much pain. When I think to be whipped, on your back and hung on a cross that lets me know by every stripe which is 39 marks tells me that I AM HEALED. Sickness, poverty, lack, sadness, shame, fear, anger, fatigue, laziness cannot attach itself to me anymore. Rejoice and renew your strength, the light of life. Do not lose your light because the enemy can take it from you. We must agree with God in order to change.

Learning how to do right depends on your decisions, so the foolishness will not appear in your life. Claim your victory. Jesus is strong, but my flesh is very weak. Use your time wisely and make adjustments to your schedule and get the proper rest you need. So you can seek God early and spend time with Him before you start your new day. Transformation has to take place and it is a life time process. Do not let people get under your skin to irritate you. We were created to be a powerful tool. Measure them up so you will know how to handle them. No need to replace God with other things, because anything else will not work. Everybody does not want to be free. Hold strong to the word and be radical, extraordinary, extremely excited, and overflowing with joy. Your joy will be increased. Your feelings will get stronger and stronger. Satan wants to put the light out and steal your joy.

Comply to keep believing in the abilities that were given to you. Trust to be happy. People will interrupt your lifestyle as much as possible to put you behind. So they can have the upper hand on you. Always seek to be conducive, productive and useful for anything that conspire to your teachings. Dictate, and justify your future so you can prepare, and establish great habits. You can release only what you have received. It feels good to be alive. We must work out our responsibility and God's role is to work in. You have to lose in order to gain; do not ever forget that. It supposed to bring us closer to Christ. Things may be in your way, but you have the power to move them out. I am nothing without sweet Jesus. You can never get enough, it will always take more of you. Great things are to be in our lives. Live out of the cage.

Know When The Spirit Speaks

Some things have to be believed to be seen. Get away from the evil spirits so it cannot attach itself to you. When people tend to not listen to me, evil things happen from different aspects and that goes the same way for me when I do not listen to others. If you do not know how to handle me, Let go. Do not let your weight hinder you from getting the job done. Balance your interests beforehand. It is totally up to you to find out who you are.

I cried out to God in anger, and bitterness, and He heard my cry. I really did not get to go to sleep until 3:00 am. But set the alarm for 6:00 am. and made it to corporate prayer to dance before the Lord. Oh how great it felt to be in God's presence. I want to be woke-up in readiness before our King. I need to enjoy who I AM. I have to use my kingdom authority. I got power and power is the ability to influence and control life's situation. Every family needs to wake-up, if we do not deposit into our children; it is going to get worse. Pride builds walls, humility builds bridges. He who kneels down to pray can stand against anything.

Know When The Spirit Speaks

Eat the best do not settle for less. If you eat the fish of the sea, vegetables of the garden, fruit of the trees, water from the fountain, your waist would be the way God shaped, and designed especially for you. We have added so much to it, and it formed some dysfunctional.- pork make you look like, just as the word speaks. Beef makes you look beefy, and tough; so as tender. God is preparing my house for Ministry. Getting my house in order it calls for so many ingredients. Specialize your healing and let people see the transformation. There is a city of sin and it will be healed. You have to move your body or it will get old, quickly. When you stop training your temple fat or bones begin to show and neither one looks good; if you are not properly trained. Keep going even though we are getting older and older. Move your muscles while you can. Why settle for someone who does not care about your well being or how you look.

ECCLECIATES 7:16-17

"Do not be overly righteous, Nor be overly wise: Why should you destroy yourself? Do not be

overly wicked, Nor be foolish: Why should you die before your time?"

All pop, shake, and roll; what you looking like over there? Can you not see the vision? Success taste so good that it makes you want to bite it. We were like Adam and Eve, trying to make a seed. You want to achieve it. Tick tock we are headed to the top, where Heaven is filled with rich crops.

To understand God's plan for us, we need to return to the beginning and think about the world He created. It was balance and order. Everything was beautiful. God wants the best for us. He has told us that He desires that *"you may prosper and be in good health, just as your soul prospers."* **- 3 JOHN 1:2**

Lead to the right place at the right time. Remind yourself that you were created in the image and likeness of God. Despise your birthright. Know that you have a divine inheritance. Keep your covenant with God, and understand the Kingdom of God is within you. Ask our Lord Jesus open your eyes so you can see which way to go, who to marry, and who to be around. You have to declare it. Stop doubting what God has said to you. Are you going to possess the promise that you are about to walk in? Go to Him and tell Him you want it, need it and you will live in it. He wants you to go a long way. One of the hardest things for us to admit is when we have done something wrong. It is even harder to worship or bless somebody when they have done something to you. Our sins have consequences. You better live up to what you are proclaiming. The devil is always going to use your weakness.

God wants your full attention not a weekend visit. Injuries happen fast, but we react faster. I know how it is to be poor while serving God. People will turn on you and hurt you. Please believe; do not doubt Jesus about anything. Decide who you will trust. Do not compare God with man because no one can do you like sweet Jesus. Keep working your seed to create your harvest.

Most people that are leading God's people are corrupt, they have lost their zeal. The church is now scared to be a leader. The reason is how the glory was handled. It does matter what you are doing, it matters what you are not doing. Am I doing it the right way now? What is sickening is we are not doing things the right way. Ask God how do you want me to do this? First, I have to get my own issues straighten out. We need to start seeking God on how He wants things done. Get yourself right.

When a man and woman make a bad decision; which involves sexual sin.

GENESIS 3:16

"God said: "I will greatly multiply thy sorrow and thy conception; in sorrow thou bring forth children; and thy desire shall be to thy husband, and he shall rule over there."

Death begins because we all were born into sin. All disorders starts in the head. People can smell sin throughout your body, if not properly taken care of. Everyone has broken the rules and laws of sin; lawlessness, iniquity, missing the mark, trespass, and unbelief. The devil will have you looking cheap, unsatisfied, degrading, and have you thinking you are doing great. When the

Lord has you looking and feeling beautiful and rich; adding unnecessary sin keeps the door closed for your dream to arrive. Death takes enjoyment away. Decay is less appealing. It traps you into trouble.

ROMANS 7:19

"For the good that I will, I do not do; but the evil I will not to do that I practice."

Your sin will surely be noticed if you do not recognize or know. If we would trust Him, He can solve our problems. I can imagine the miracles God have waiting. When I am released from the hand of the wickedness. His blood from death redeems, it brings us nigh, it makes peace, it justifies and it cleanses. Jesus is special because of the Holy Spirit. He wants to give His love, grace and mercy.

When Jesus came:

LUKE 19:10

"The Son of man is come to seek and to save that which was lost."

Please do not let sin keep you from reading the Bible. God will do what He said He will do. He does not lie. We all are associated with the same disease; which is sin. Our sins need to die physically to the Spirit of God. I am so tired of playing both sides of the fence. Only one side can hold me up which is the right side.

Faith Going In

Motivation from Me to You

This is the day when I came out of Egypt from a house of slavery (insufficiency, debt and lack.) God brought me out with a powerful hand and He can do the same for you. Trust Him every step of the way and follow the plan he has for your life. Living in your purpose will cause your destiny to be fulfilled. The Lord led me to **Exodus 13:3** in the message Bible: I have never been the same.

Exodus 13:3

Moses said, "Always remember this day in which you were brought out of bondage." Only by the hands of the LORD I was also delivered!

JEREMIAH 29:11

"For I know the thoughts that I think toward you, says the Lord, thoughts of peace and not of evil, to give you a future and a hope." -

Annette Alexander

<u>Acknowledgments</u>

My mother Annie Alexander
I give acknowledgment to my dearest mother who has always stood by my side no matter what. She is a woman who fights through it all. The things she taught me helped me to conquer my strong mountains that I faced. My mother is much needed in my life. I couldn't have made it without her behind me pushing, nurturing and providing me love.

To my Gift from God: My daughter's
Mikezia motivates me to higher levels of help with a shift of great inspiration that's happened during our untimely circumstances. You are my "Gift" from my heavenly father.

My aunt Yvonne
Thank you for coming to me for spiritual motivation and advice even in the storms of her life.

To all
Take a step of FAITH and all losses will stop! Have FAITH IN GOD ... I NEED GOD'S FAVOR and NOTHING ELSE MATTERS.

From my loving aunt Yvonne:

Annette Alexander is one of the most inspiration women in my life. She is one of Charlotte's greatest uprising newest Entrepreneurs, who stands by her Faith, as she stands by her beliefs. May you always be successful in your passions in life and in God. She is one of God's children. To me she is a Politician for God. So keep on campaigning for HIM. As a mother, daughter, sister, niece, or friend you can always get her support where and when needed. She lets you know that God is always there at your highest or lowest moments. All you have to do is believe. So, Annette keep on walking in Faith.

Your Loving Aunt Yvonne.

Faith Going In

To contact the author
Annette Alexander

Email: faithcleaningsvc@yahoo.com

Website:

www.faithcleaningsvc.com

Know When The Spirit Speaks

www.ingramcontent.com/pod-product-compliance
Lightning Source LLC
Chambersburg PA
CBHW051727090426
42738CB00010B/2124